I don't Want to Take My Medicine!

JENNIFER GROFF

Gotham Books
30 N Gould St.
Ste. 20820, Sheridan, WY 82801
https://gothambooksinc.com/

Phone: 1 (307) 464-7800

Published by Gotham Books (June 24, 2022)

ISBN: 978-1-956349-89-4 (sc)
ISBN: 978-1-956349-90-0 (e)

I dedicate this book to
my husband Daniel,
my family Dale,
Darren, Isabella,
Julian, and
Dr. Samantha Morrow

One Friday morning Chad woke up with a sore throat and a fever. Mary, Chad's mom tried to get him to take medicine that would lower his fever and take some of the pain away from his throat, but he refused. Mary then called the doctor to schedule an appointment.
She scheduled the appointment for 10:00 that day.

Chad told his mom that he really did not want to go to the doctor because she always gives him medicine. He did not like taking medicine. He replied to his mom, "I don't want to take medicine! It doesn't taste good!"

It's 9:15 and it was time for Mary to get Chad ready to go see the doctor. When they arrived at the doctor's office, Mary signed Chad in. He is seeing Dr. Morrow today. Then they had a seat in the waiting room until they called out Chad's name.

When they called Chad's name, his first stop was getting on the scale to check his height and weight and to see how much he has grown. He then walked back to a room where they waited to see Dr. Morrow.

Dr. Morrow comes into the room and greets Chad and his mother. Dr. Morrow is amazed at the growth that Chad has made since his last visit. "Boy did you grow! You grew three inches and gained four pounds."

Dr. Morrow then asks Chad to tell her why he is coming to see her. Chad starts to talk and says "Ouch!" Chad finds it difficult to talk because of how much his throat hurts. Dr. Morrow then asks his mom what the problem is other than his throat. She said that he was also running a fever of 101°. Dr. Morrow explained that the fever is letting you know that he is not feeling well and that explains his throat hurting. After Dr. Morrow examined Chad, she confirmed that he had a sore throat because it was red.

Dr. Morrow explained to Mary that Chad needed to take a course of antibiotics and another medication to help him get better. She then wrote the names of the prescribed medication down for Mary to take to the pharmacy.

Dr. Morrow explained to Chad that there are many different ways to take a pill. She then shared her way of taking a pill. Dr. Morrow explained and demonstrated how to take a pill by taking a drink of water and dropping a small piece of candy into her mouth and swallowing them. The candy disappeared.

Chad worried the whole time about what kind of medicine he was getting. He didn't like the taste of the liquid medicine and he was just learning how to swallow a pill. On the way to the pharmacy where they had to get Chad's medicine, he kept asking what type of medicine he was having to take. Mom knew the name of the medicine, but was unsure how he had to take it.

When Mary and Chad got to the pharmacy, Mary handed in the prescriptions to the pharmacist and had to wait. While waiting, they went to the Candy aisle to pick up some small candy that Chad could practice with.

The pharmacist called Chad's name and it was time for him to pick up his prescriptions. Chad's mom paid for the medicine and candy and was told how to give the medicine. Chad was still looking worried about how to take the medicine. He thought "there's no good way to take it."

When Chad got home he started to cry. He was so upset that he had two medicines that he had to take. His mom explained to him that he had a liquid and a pill. His mom was willing to try anything for him to take his medicine.

Chad's mom said let's look up on the computer to see if there are any other ways suggested to take medicine so you can get well soon.

When they searched on the internet, they found several new ways that they have never tried before. Suggestions for liquid medicines.

1. Eat a piece of chocolate to coat your mouth, then take the liquid medicine. The taste should be hidden with the flavor and thickness of the chocolate residue.

2. Try drinking a frozen drink to make the mouth cold and then take the liquid medicine and follow up with another swallow of the frozen drink. The cold and flavor should hide the taste of the medicine

3. Use a dropper so that you can aim it towards the back of your throat more to make it easier and quicker to swallow.

4. Close your eyes and hold your nose and swallow.

Ways to make it easier to swallow a pill.

1. Practice by swallowing small pieces of candy.
2. Dip the pill into something wet to make it more slipperier.
3. Place the pill into a bite of pudding.
4. Take a drink of water, drop the pill into the back of the mouth, and swallow.
5. Mix it into a food like applesauce.
6. Open mouth, line pill up front to back near the back of the mouth, take a drink and swallow.

Chad was very excited to hear all of the options. Mary allowed Chad to choose one way. He was in charge this time of taking his medicine and he knew what he was going to do for each kind.

For the awful tasting liquid medicine Chad chose to eat a piece of chocolate then take the medicine. He was amazed at how it helped. It hid the awful taste. Next was the hard one. He got that lump in your throat feeling. He just started taking pills because Dr. Morrow said that he was old enough to. He didn't feel ready.

Keeping with the chocolate theme, he decided to try taking the pill with chocolate pudding. He had to think about this because he put the pill in the container and forgot where he put it. Now he had to just try it and if he felt it in his mouth, he knew what to do.

He took the first spoonful and there was nothing. The second spoonful, nothing. Finally, the third spoonful, he felt something in his mouth and swallowed. He didn't panic, he was prepared and swallowed. It went right down without any issues.

His mom was so proud of him! He took both of his medicines without complaining and was confident about his choice of method to take his medicine.

A few days had passed and he was starting to feel better. He tried a couple different ways to take his medicine, but his mom let him in charge and he was successful. Chad found the method that he liked, and he stuck with it.

When he was better, he had to go back to Dr. Morrow just to make sure everything was back to normal. The doctor asked Chad how it went taking his medicine and he replied, "Great!" Dr. Morrow was not expecting that kind of response. She was curious about what he did. Chad explained to her that he and his mom looked things up on the internet and tried some of the suggestions until he liked one of them. Dr. Morrow was so proud of him for taking charge in taking his medicine to get well.

He and his mom were thankful to Dr. Morrow for giving him the correct medicine to get him to feel well fast.

Chad was thankful that now he has several different ways to take medicine if he needs to.

Printed in the USA
CPSIA information can be obtained
at www.ICGtesting.com
LVHW072342121123
763741LV00052BA/1401